How NOT *To Make Love To A Woman*

How NOT To Make Love To A Woman

by G. Gaynor McTigue

ISBN 0-7871-1031-0
Printed in the United States of America

Dove Books
8955 Beverly Boulevard
West Hollywood, CA 90048

Distributed by Penguin USA

Text design and layout by Once Upon a Design

G. Gaynor McTigue can be reached for questions and comments by e-mail at: jerrym321@aol.com
Web site: http://members.aol.com/jerrym321/books.htm

First Printing: October 1996

10   9   8   7   6   5   4   3   2   1

Introduction

❤

What does a woman really want in a relationship with a man?

Who knows? But as someone who has keenly observed the vast gulf between expectation and reality, I can certainly tip you off to what she *doesn't* want.

Sure, there are tons of serious books out there that exhort men to be caring, sensitive, and sweet. But how many guys who could most use this advice do you see reading them?

Here's a book designed to grab the attention of even the most brain-dead of lovers. And if it takes a little irreverent humor to drum home the message, so be it.

So girls, allow your man a few indulgent chuckles for the greater good.

And guys, have some fun with this. But remember, the operative word here is *not.* This is How *Not* to Make Love to a Woman.

Got it? Enjoy!

—*G. Gaynor McTigue*

1. Inform her that if she can find the pendant in your chest hair, she gets you for the night.

2. Always steer the conversation back to yourself.

3. Wear no deodorant, in the hope she'll be turned on by your natural body odor.

4. Undress her with your eyes, then ask to see how accurate you were.

5. Answer her personal ad with shots of you in the buff.

6. Go for the onions, even though she doesn't.

7. Fall asleep on top of her.

8. Look her directly in the cleavage when she's talking to you.

9. Demonstrate your manliness by cursing out the waiter in her presence.

10. Wear briefs that say "Come to me, Mama!" across the front.

11. French kiss her at dawn, while she's still asleep.

12. Ogle a Victoria's Secret catalog in her presence.

13. Surprise her with a Dustbuster for Valentine's Day.

14. When she asks you to apply suntan lotion, take it to mean "feel me up."

15. Sign your anniversary card "From."

16. When she tells you she loves you, say thank you.

17. Lick your lips liberally before your first kiss.

18. Skip the foreplay and go for the gold.

19. Scream "It's going . . . going . . . gone!" at orgasm.

20. Send her home in a cab so you can meet the boys for a nightcap.

21. Check yourself out repeatedly in store windows as you stroll together down the street.

22. . . . and be sure to turn around and survey the rear of attractive women who pass by.

23. Replace the gold Cartier watch she gave you with a cheap knockoff, then pocket the difference.

24. Introduce her to others as your "woman."

25. Place both hands on her buttocks during your first slow dance.

26. Get in the car first (especially if it's raining), then reach over and unlock her door.

27. Go on and on about the wonderful attributes of your mother.

28. Proudly show her your Joey Buttafuoco scrapbook.

29. Have your secretary call to ask for a date.

30. Laugh when she cries during a tender scene in the movie.

31. Ask her what the real color of her hair is.

32. Ask her what the original shape of her nose was.

33. Introduce her to your parents as Bachelorette #3.

34. Inquire: "What's a pretty little thing like you doing at a high-powered business conference like this?"

35. Tell her you're an ardent supporter of women's lib. And to pick you up at seven.

36. Run your fingers through her hair . . . *before* you go out.

37. Bring a case of Old Milwaukee to her black-tie dinner party.

38. Lavish her with zircons . . . she'll never know the difference.

39. Demonstrate how accurately you can spit tobacco juice.

40. Take her to the most romantic restaurant in town . . . fervently propose to her . . . then pull out the pre-nup.

41. Wear more jewelry than she does.

42. While she's undressing, reach over and give her a wedgie.

43. Attribute her mistakes to gender.

44. Show up at her door shirtless, like Sly Stallone would.

45. Cry "Huff and puff, my little honey bunny," during labor.

46. Complain that her Chanel No. 5 clashes with your Aqua Velva.

47. Floss at the dinner table.

48. Brush your crumbs over to her side of the bed.

49. Flex your pecs at every opportunity.

50. Fly her down to your yacht in the Bahamas for a weekend of fun with you and your other girlfriends.

51. Show her your softer side. Play "This Little Piggy" on her foot.

52. Borrow huge sums of money from her.

53. Wear a hair net to bed.

54. As she's leaving your apartment the next morning, ask her to sign the guest book.

55. . . . and tell her you'd appreciate any comments, too.

56. Share with her your passion for watching insects fry on the bug zapper.

57. Take long romantic walks with just the two of you . . . and your cellular phone.

58. Bring your binoculars to the beach.

59. Break wind frequently and unabashedly during moments of intimacy.

60. When she asks why you haven't called in weeks, say you forgot.

61. Demonstrate how expertly you can undo a bra with one hand.

62. Bring her to meet the gang down at the arcade.

63. Feel comfortable enough in your relationship to pick your nose in her presence . . .

64. . . . drop your laundry off at her place . . .

65. . . . brush lint off her bosom . . .

66. . . . and reveal your secret life as an Elvis impersonator.

67. Point out attributes in other women you'd like her to emulate.

68. Stick a wet finger in her ear.

69. When she wants to know how you feel about her, use words like "groovy."

70. Call her collect.

71. Swagger into the bedroom in your Wallace Beary underwear.

72. Every time you say good-bye, add "Here's looking at you, kid."

73. Post detailed accounts of her sexual prowess, and her phone number, on the Internet.

74. When she asks you what you're thinking . . . tell her the truth.

75. Videotape your lovemaking, then point out areas that could use improvement.

76. Bring out the big guns for your evening of seduction: incense, lava lamps, and Barry Manilow records.

77. When she regrets she'll be busy Saturday night, ask to speak to her roommate.

78. Laugh a little too indulgently at Andrew Dice Clay monologues.

79. Go ahead, be a romantic and take her to a museum. Cooperstown.

80. When you pick her up, give her a choice: She can have her "dessert" now . . . or after the tractor pull.

81. Make your pitch by complimenting her amplitude in the hooter department.

82. Inject a little levity into her bridal shower by streaking through the living room.

83. Wait for the most romantic moment in the evening to make your impassioned declaration: "I'm horny as a toad."

84. Interrupt your lovemaking to remove your teeth, contacts, and toupee.

85. Make her get out of the warm bed to turn off the light.

86. Relate the details of your recent bout of diarrhea at the dinner table.

87. Then order for her the black bean soup.

88. Give her a cheek burn with your five o'clock shadow.

89. Tell her father his daughter is one voluptuous fox.

90. Tell her mother that if she were 30 years younger . . .

91. While she's lying face down at the beach with her bikini top unstrapped, pour ice water on her back.

92. Then introduce yourself.

93. When she snuggles up close and says "Light my fire, lover boy," tell her your apartment is a smoke-free environment.

94. Scoff at her when she tries to convince you professional wrestling isn't real.

95. Propose as your wedding song: "What's Love Got To Do With It?"

96. Do a Marv Albert play-by-play of your first lovemaking interlude.

97. Invite her over to look at your baby pictures.

98. Bogart the covers.

99. Book you, her, and your ex-wife on *Geraldo.*

100. Quietly slip out of her apartment at 3 A.M.

101. While whispering tender endearments in her ear . . . sneeze.

102. Tease her on April Fool's Day with a drive-by moon.

103. Invite her to a party, then hang out with the guys in the kitchen all night.

104. Express a burning desire to make love to her on your horsehair couch.

105. For her birthday, hire a male stripper to perform at her office.

106. Ask her if she'd like to make a few extra bucks cleaning your apartment.

107. When she expresses a desire to strengthen the bonds of your relationship, tie her to the bedpost.

108. Declare yourself to be bisexual. That is, you prefer to have sex with two women at the same time.

109. Adopt as a stock reply to her amorous advances: "Wait'll half-time, Honey."

110. Titter, giggle, and blush when she's introduced to you.

111. Comment on her interesting network of character lines.

112. Stand her up on the first date, just to keep her off stride.

113. Pose the hypothetical question: "If you were a sexual position, what would you be?"

114. Give her a complete rundown on the week's results of your computer baseball league.

115. When she inquires if you're seeing other women, ask if that includes girly magazines.

116. Deck yourself out in your finest double-knit leisure suit for her company picnic.

117. Inquire: "Was it good for you?"

118. Envelop her in sensuous cigar smoke.

119. Complain that your last girlfriend had the nerve to suggest you bathe daily.

120. Wear wraparound mirrored shades to establish your cool.

121. Sitting across from her on the bus, try as an opener: "I see London, I see France . . . "

122. Hit her with your favorite knock-knock jokes.

123. When she suggests a little S&M, respond that baked beans leave you flatulent.

124. Wear your jockstrap *over* your sweatpants.

125. Point out that your mother always made *her* cakes from scratch.

126. Ask: "Are they real, or are they silicone?"

127. Work the starving artist angle to get her to pay.

128. Call her at four in the morning and whisper, "A penny for your thoughts."

129. Tell her she's got a heck of a lot of opinions for a lady.

130. Ask her to fax you a 3-month schedule of her period so you won't have to waste any dates.

131. Spend more on your dog's gift than hers.

132. Rely frequently on the "If you really love me . . ." ploy to get what you want.

133. While taking a shower together, flick off the hot and jump out.

134. Wax intelligent on the less obvious aspects of cockfighting.

135. Send her disparaging birthday cards that you think are funny.

136. Forget her name.

137. Get seasick on her waterbed.

138. Coat yourself in oil and ask her if she'd like a cucumber salad.

139. Fill the peaceful night air with loud, obnoxious snoring.

140. Go ballistic when she schedules the wedding on your bowling night.

141. E-mail your Dear John letter.

142. Attribute her loathing of your oversized tires to penis envy.

143. Periodically critique her in three key areas: sex, housekeeping, and food service.

144. Take her on a whirlwind courtship of roller derby, biker bars, and repossessed auto auctions.

145. Make jokes about married people.

146. In the throes of orgasm tell her you love her, then request that it be struck from the record.

147. Beep her when horny.

148. Describe the romance and adventure of life together in a trailer park.

149. Bring her back to your place and throw your roommates out of the bedroom.

150. Have her drop you off at the restaurant while she looks for a parking space.

151. Tell her you waited a long time for a woman worthy enough to share your half-price Denny's coupon with.

152. Puzzle about former Senator Bob Packwood: "What'd the guy do that was so bad?"

153. Gripe, "Who do I look like, Arnold Schwarzenegger?" when she asks you to carry her across the threshold.

154. Express intimate feelings through body language: Snap your fingers and point to your crotch.

155. When she asks if you like kids, answer: "Yeah. Other people's."

156. Join her workout class so you can watch her do pelvic thrusts.

157. Reassure her with the words: "A dame like you could do a lot worse than a guy like me."

158. Illuminate your bedroom with bright, flattering fluorescent light.

159. Seat her in the restaurant facing the wall.

160. . . . so you can look out and flirt with other women during the meal.

161. Cynically introduce her to others as your first wife.

162. Wear pants that accentuate your "package."

163. Ask her to do a 360° in front of your male friends.

164. Make no effort to hide your disappointment the first time you see her in broad daylight.

165. When she runs out of depilatory cream, offer to lend her yours.

166. Start arguments in restaurants.

167. Arrange a romantic weekend escape at Motel 6.

168. Sing "Besame Mucho" beneath her bedroom window.

169. Make it clear that the engagement ring is a loaner.

170. Leave a pair of handcuffs on the night table and see if she takes the hint.

171. Get her one present annually to cover birthday, Christmas, Valentine's Day and anniversary.

172. Comment on how comfy-cozy it is in bed with you, her, and your stuffed animals.

173. When the singing guitarist strolls over to your table, tell him to take a hike.

174. Always leave the toilet seat up.

175. When she's not looking, replace the restaurant fortune cookie with an X-rated one.

176. Pardoning your curiosity, ask her if she's going gray down below, too.

177. Constantly direct while she's driving.

178. Every time you say you're sorry, qualify it with a "but."

179. Tout your expertise in frontal body massage.

180. When you establish eye contact across a crowded room, nod politely . . . smile warmly . . . then flutter your tongue at her.

181. Greet her with: "How's my favorite little plaything?"

182. Be really bummed out that she makes more money than you do.

183. Rarely, if ever, "get it."

184. Invite her to a party at your house, then pretend no one else showed up.

185. Compliment her on how mature she looks for her age.

186. Promise her anything . . . but give her a Chia Pet.

187. Make her feel like one of the guys. Tell her your filthiest jokes.

188. Crochet her a shawl.

189. Flaunt your oversized paunch like it's a life achievement.

190. Floor her with your Joe Cocker impersonation at the karaoke bar.

191. Describe yourself as a soap-on-a-rope kind of guy.

192. When she excitedly hints there may be a bassinet in your future, tell her you aren't musically inclined.

193. Invite her up to share a Sleepytime Tea moment.

194. During a romantic after-dinner stroll, buy a single rose from a street vendor . . . sniff its sweet bouquet . . . break off the stem . . . and stick it in your lapel.

195. Endeavor to win her heart with your favorite poetry: "There once was a man from Nantucket . . . "

196. Ask her why she can't be more like those obedient girls from the East.

197. Totally ignore her for a week, then get all lovey-dovey when you "want it."

198. Let it be known through a mutual friend you've got "hot rocks" for her.

199. Leer at her as she moves around the kitchen.

200. Wear the T-shirt: "Life's a bitch. Then you marry one."

201. Fast dance like a freak.

202. Get all bent out of shape when she playfully touches your hair.

203. Casually dismiss as a myth the pain of childbirth.

204. Relate the details of your erotic dream, starring her best friend.

205. When she calls your shared workspace to continue an argument, put her on speakerphone.

206. Whisper "How 'bout a hug, Honey?" expelled on the wings of morning breath.

207. If she isn't ready on time, leave without her.

208. Goof on her relatives.

209. Yawn, look at your watch, stare into space . . . anything but focus on her.

210. Rather than comment on what she buys, always ask: "How much did it cost?"

211. Be cocky, arrogant, and gruff. After all, that's what a woman wants, isn't it?

212. Suspend all romantic activity when "Beavis and Butt-head" comes on.

213. Try to look up her dress as you're helping her out of the car.

214. Blame her for all your failures . . . especially the ones she had nothing to do with.

215. Let her carry her *own* drink to the restaurant table.

216. Balk childishly when she asks for a bite of your entree.

217. Wear your jacket and tie around the house.

218. Wear your mesh shirt to the church social.

219. Spend half of your honeymoon on the phone with your office.

220. Always drive with one hand on her thigh.

221. Fire her.

222. Leave the mess for her to clean up.

223. Dump your emotional baggage on her lap each evening.

224. Ask if she wouldn't mind being your good luck charm down at the pool hall.

225. Make jokes about her ethnicity.

226. Express disgust that she's had other lovers, even though you have, too.

227. Take "I will love, honor, and obey him" literally.

228. Call her up to say you'd like to get her on your calendar.

229. Always enter the restaurant first.

230. Grab the last seat on the bus for yourself, particularly if she's pregnant.

231. Belch while kissing.

232. Bring your mother along on the honeymoon.

233. After talking about yourself all evening, open it up to questions.

234. Attribute your children's positive traits to your family, and their negative traits to hers.

235. Suavely sidle up behind her and wrap your cold hands around her bare waist.

236. To others, refer to her as "the wife."

237. Find fault in everything she does.

238. Run a background check on her.

239. Address your Valentine card to her, or "current resident."

240. Slow dance to fast songs.

241. While taking your marital vows . . . faint.

242. Blow your nose like a foghorn.

243. Put on soft music, turn the lights down low, take her gently by the hand . . . and duck walk.

244. Emphasize things you have in common. Like genitals.

245. When she asks who your best previous lover was, hold up your hand.

246. Proudly introduce her to your bevy of inflatable beauties.

247. Whenever she asks a favor, say "Sure," then mutter under your breath, "Bitch."

248. While you're doing the talking, let your fingers do the walking.

249. Your long-term goal in life? Instant gratification.

250. When picking her up, park in front of the house and lean on the horn a few minutes.

251. Remember, every woman secretly yearns to be thrown into the ocean while the entire beach looks on.

252. Answer her well-founded complaints with: "So sue me."

253. Upchuck the gourmet dinner she cooked for you.

254. Take up body painting, then suggest that she be your canvas.

255. Wail during sappy TV commercials.

256. Hyperventilate when she mentions the word "commitment."

257. Read a magazine during foreplay.

258. Take an active interest in her appearance: Buy her fake eyelashes, falsies, and a wig.

259. When she joyously breaks the news that she's pregnant, respond: "Is it mine?"

260. Fail to mention you have a wife and kids.

261. Be a father figure to her: crass, inattentive, and demanding.

262. Affirm your belief in more traditional values. Like dowries.

263. Make as your first sexual overture: "Naughty little girls need to be spanked."

264. Reveal as little about your feelings as humanly possible.

265. Get drunk and pass out on your wedding night.

266. Concede that her accomplishments aren't too shabby. For a woman.

267. Hit on your sister-in-law.

268. Avoid boring preliminaries by handing out question-naires: *"What's your name? What do you do? Where are you from? What's your sign? . . . "*

269. Propose that your first face-to-face be coffee at the Hilton. Then if things work out, you can go right upstairs.

270. If she flirts with the waiter, you do likewise.

271. Insist on a crab check before you have sex.

272. Shrug your shoulders, avert your eyes, and mumble inaudibly when you answer, "I love you, too."

273. Make it clear that what you most want from your relationship . . . is a surrogate mother.

274. Share the household duties: She cooks, cleans, launders, and irons; you take out the garbage.

275. When she returns from the ladies' room on your first date, ask, "Was it a onesy, or a twosy?"

276. As background music on your answering machine, play "I'm too sexy for my shirt."

277. Put a "take a number" machine next to where you're standing at the singles bar.

278. Sure, you'd love to go away with her for the weekend. But you have to check with your parole officer first.

279. Declare your favorite movie to be *The Stepford Wives.*

280. Try to seduce her when she's sick.

281. Reveal that you're still in therapy over John Lennon's death.

282. If a little cologne works well, a whole lot is even better!

283. Join the anti-fur movement, just to avoid having to buy her one.

284. When she looks lovingly into your eyes, stare her down.

285. Drop subtle hints about your colossal length.

286. Hoist your smelly feet onto her lap.

287. Tweak her nipples.

288. Call her up half-bagged at 2 A.M. and ask if you can "stop by for a while."

289. Make loud, explosive noises on the stool.

290. Have an extramarital affair with the cleaning lady.

291. After you unceremoniously dump her, add: "We can still be friends."

292. Deride her for throwing like a girl.

293. Make out with her in public places.

294. Subscribe to the theory that when a woman says no, she really means yes.

295. Go no farther than the corner drugstore to buy her a gift.

296. Tell her anything, if it will help you score.

297. When she gives you the ultimatum, "Love me or leave me," do both.

298. Make goofy faces in your wedding pictures.

299. Divulge her innermost secrets . . . to the plumber.

300. Send her out for ice cream at 1 A.M.

301. Fall asleep on her shoulder . . . and drool all over her.

302. Complain about her personal hygiene to your guests.

303. Tap her phone line.

304. Let your shirt-pocket pens jab her in the chest when you embrace.

305. As long as she's paying for the wedding, go whole hog.

306. Hang out in places where you might meet someone with similar interests. Like the lingerie department.

307. Shine your Itty Bitty Book Light in her face.

308. If you get your entree first, go ahead and start eating.

309. When she says, "Don't make a fuss on my birthday" . . . don't.

310. Never go anywhere without your baseball cap.

311. Praise that beautiful naked body in front of you. Then turn away from the mirror and jump into the sack.

312. Compliment her cute mustache.

313. When you hear noises in the night, send her down to investigate.

314. Threaten to drown a kitten if she doesn't go out with you.

315. Make lip-smacking noises when you eat.

316. Clip your toenails in bed.

317. Hang out, jabbering away in the kitchen, while she's trying to prepare for dinner guests.

318. When you call her up for a date, ask her what brand of condoms she prefers.

319. Crash her tupperware party.

320. Dock her house allowance for lackluster sex.

321. Describe in phantasmagoric detail your epic dreams.

322. When she indicates she doesn't care for fellatio, concur that he's not one of your favorite Shakespearean characters, either.

323. Suggest conjugal visits to your office.

324. Get caught rifling through her underwear at the Laundromat.

325. Roust her out of bed with a bugle.

326. Complete her sentences for her.

327. Arrive for dates early, in the hope you'll catch her in her bra and panties.

328. If the relationship doesn't work out, maybe you could interest her in an Amway distributorship.

329. Leave little notes around the house for things you want her to do.

330. Say: "I like your qualifications already," before you interview her for a job.

331. Be cheerful, loud, and perky first thing in the morning.

332. Dismiss her practical advice as "old wives' tales."

333. Never show any affection for her in public.

334. Categorically refuse to pick up tampons at the drugstore.

335. Routinely tune her out when she's talking to you.

336. Once you're married, feel free to open her mail.

337. When she says she could really go for a Slurpee, lay a wet one on her.

338. Accede to her wishes and rent a steamy movie for Saturday night: *The Towering Inferno.*

339. If your eyes are the windows to your soul, wear shades.

340. When she confides that her father can't stand you, suggest a buyout.

341. Be the strong, silent type. Passing gas, that is.

342. Stop abruptly in the middle of lovemaking to say you ran into an old buddy of yours.

343. Now that you're engaged, you can go back to being a slob again.

344. Liken her personality to that of a mackerel.

345. Pick out the one minor glitch in an otherwise perfect dinner and harp on it.

346. When you smell a poop in your toddler's diaper, say "Go see Mommy."

347. Tell her you'd like to start dating other women (even though you're married).

348. Call up her old boyfriends for tips on getting her into the sack.

349. Be the one who starts conga lines at parties.

350. Make her ask something two or three times before you respond.

351. Let it only serve to strengthen your resolve when she says, "Get lost, jerk."

352. Lambada with her maid of honor at your wedding reception.

353. Moan when beautiful women appear on the TV screen.

354. Send her those cheap generic greeting cards you get free in the mail from charities.

355. Bring your boss home for dinner . . . unannounced . . . on leftover night.

356. Wipe your face after she kisses you.

357. Leave her in the middle of the dance floor.

358. Tell her she broke into your top 40 list of great lays.

359. Ask for references.

360. Demonstrate your helpfulness by trying to smooth away her panty lines.

361. Offer as a birthday gift anything she wants from the Playboy Catalog.

362. After you're married, institute a dress code.

363. Adopt as your standard pitch line: "Wanna get lucky tonight?"

364. Tell her your relationship has a storybook ending. It's over.

365. . . . but you wouldn't mind one last roll in the hay.